NEW QUEER CONSCIENCE

For my grandmothers Freda Braunstein,
Rita Werner, and all of the women, queer and not,
Jewish and not, who make the world go around—AE

PENGUIN WORKSHOP
An Imprint of Penguin Random House LLC, New York

Text copyright © 2020 by Adam Eli Werner. Illustrations copyright © 2020 by Penguin Random House LLC. All rights reserved. Published by Penguin Workshop, an imprint of Penguin Random House LLC, New York. PENGUIN and PENGUIN WORKSHOP are trademarks of Penguin Books Ltd, and the W colophon is a registered trademark of Penguin Random House LLC. Manufactured in China.

Visit us online at www.penguinrandomhouse.com.

Library of Congress Cataloging-in-Publication Data is available upon request.

ISBN 9780593093689   10 9 8 7 6 5 4 3

PROLOGUE

On October 27, 2018, a gunman burst into a Pittsburgh synagogue and killed eleven people. Within hours, the global Jewish community mobilized into action. Jews across the world raised money to cover funeral costs. Rallies and memorials were held in every major city. The global Jewish community expressed public sympathy and outrage, while volunteers flocked to Pittsburgh to serve the community hot meals and attend the funerals. The message was clear: An attack on one of us is an attack on all of us.

In general, the global queer community does not respond like this in times of crisis. On January 14, 2019, just two and a half months after the synagogue shooting, news broke that a new wave of queer "purges" were taking place in Chechnya, a small Russian republic. Forty queer people were detained and two were killed. But there was no effective global call to action. Between October 27 and January 14, at least three Black trans women were murdered in the United States. As usual, the epidemic of violence against Black trans women did not prompt any kind of unified or helpful communal outrage.

As a queer Jew, I watched these attacks on my two communities unfold parallel to each other. Distraught, I thought of a quote from the Talmud, a piece of ancient Jewish scripture, that says, "All Jewish people are responsible for one another." We don't always get it right, but the importance of showing up for other Jews has been carved into the DNA of what it means to be Jewish. It is my dream that queer people develop the same ideology—what I like to call a Global Queer Conscience. The Global Queer Conscience is an attitude that repositions how we see ourselves as queer people and how we fit into the world.

I cannot, and will not, speak for the community

at large—no one person can. But I believe that this dream will become reality if we come to this simple understanding:

Queer people anywhere are responsible for queer people everywhere.

THE NEW QUEER CONSCIENCE

I wish someone had told me that being queer means you are never alone.

It is 10:15 p.m. I am sixteen years old and in the worst pain of my life. I am in love with my straight best friend. I am standing at a party in total shock as he gives me a play-by-play of his first hookup with his new girlfriend. I act curious and excited, demanding all the details.

At some point, I grab his shoulder, eager for any kind of contact with him. He shrugs me off, and I disappear toward the train home.

My heart rate rises. I can no longer speak. I'm standing at the train station. Flashes of our conversation: his face, her hands, his zipper. I double over clutching my stomach. I tell myself, as I always I do, that if I replay the scene in my mind it will eventually hurt less.

Pulse, mind, and tears racing, I'm sure she doesn't see his beauty the way I do. But a wave of nausea and pain forces me to refocus. Her hand, his Abercrombie & Fitch jeans, a zipper . . . and blackout.

The next day in algebra he throws me an

encouraging wink as our teacher distributes a midterm. An unintentional kick to the stomach. I flee to the bathroom and lock the door.

Big picture, I don't know anyone queer who can tell me that these feelings are normal. And from a practical perspective, nobody can tell me anything because I just locked myself in the bathroom.

So, I turn on the tap and speak to myself. I look in the mirror and say out loud, for the first time, "Adam Eli, you are gay . . ." I let that sentence echo a little in the bathroom, for the drama. Then I hear words not of my making, but out loud, in my own voice, address the mirror:

". . . and it's going to be okay."

What does queer mean?

I am gay because I primarily experience same-sex attraction, and, by my own definition, that also makes me queer. Many people have their own definition of what queer means, and one is no more valid than another, but here is mine:

Queer: different, or other

If there are three blue chairs and one pink chair—the pink chair is queer. Queerness only exists in opposition to what's perceived as "normal." When it comes to gender and sexuality, our society's "normal" is defined by one cisgender man and one cisgender woman who experience opposite-sex attraction and live comfortably in their gender roles. If you deviate from any part of that norm, welcome and pull up a seat. In my book, you are queer!

When describing our community, I always say LGBTQIAA+ (lesbian, gay, bisexual, trans, queer, intersex, asexual, ally, plus). The most important of these symbols is the plus sign. The plus sign opens the door for everyone. Perhaps you do not identify with any of these letters. Perhaps how you feel or how you are has not been verbalized to the world yet. You are loved, and you are welcome here.

The word *queer* and the community it describes are both evolving—and that's a good thing. I hope our community continues to expand and becomes more inclusive in ways that I cannot predict. I imagine, and hope, that one day my definition will be outdated.

When I was younger, I knew I was different because all my interests were "meant for" girls. I was obsessed with Disney princesses and had a huge crush on Leonardo DiCaprio in *Titanic*. If I could have pressed a button to become more like my female friends, I would have in a heartbeat.

I was resentful and confused. Uncomfortable with boys and forbidden to be one of the girls, I existed in the margins, in a space between spaces.

I grew up in an Orthodox Jewish community, and every Saturday, when my family attended our synagogue, I would sneak from the boys' youth group to the girls'. But even in the relative safety of my female friends, I couldn't relax. I was always on alert for older boys who may come over to call me my least favorite word—"GAY."

Gay.

I grew up in a community without a single person who openly identified as queer. But from the moment I heard the word *gay*, I knew those boys were right. The word hit me physically, like a heavy monster that was squeezing me from behind. I felt unfairly exposed. I didn't choose to be gay, and I certainly didn't choose to live in a world where I couldn't express it. Why was I being punished for both?

So, like many other queer people, I began to hide pieces of myself. And the adults around me followed suit. My father bought me dolls and a Barbie Dreamhouse, but we hid it when guests came over. My mother bought me every young adult book aimed at girls, but she also bought Book Sox to wrap the covers and conceal what I was reading. Only my brothers knew about the dolls and the books. They kept our family secret and made sure the taunting at school was kept to a minimum, or at least to when I was out of earshot. While entirely unintentional, my family's actions sent a clear message: We see you as you are. We love you as you are. But let's keep that hidden for now.

As I grew, so did my secrets. In high school, I didn't tell anyone I was in love with my best friend. We had the type of intimacy pretty standard for teenage boys. We'd share secrets, have sleepovers, but would never undress in front of each other. When he talked about girls and the things he was doing with them, it felt like someone had condensed a ball of energy and shoved it down my throat where it whirled and raged in my stomach.

Of course, all of my friends had their hearts broken, too. I had seen *Mean Girls*. I knew unrequited teenage love didn't make me special or unique. But as my straight friends supported one another through breakups, crushes, and the rest, I simply didn't have that luxury. I was left alone to manage a storm of feelings that were volatile at best and terrifying at worst.

But even then, I knew that I was pretty lucky as far as closeted teenagers go. I understood what was happening around me—these emotional and physical feelings meant I was a homosexual, and I knew that being a homosexual didn't make me a bad person.

I also knew that my school and community were not safe places for me to come out.

Above all, I understood that I couldn't spend too much time focusing on the injustice of the situation, or when and how I was going to come out. I had to put every ounce of energy into surviving the day. Or else I wouldn't.

One of the reasons being in the closet is so painful is that it seems like you're the only person in the world feeling what you're feeling. How are you supposed to know that something is normal if you can't talk about it or don't hear about it from other people?

What I failed to understand was that my queer experience was not singular. I was one of *many* queer kids feeling alone and trapped.

After coming out in college, I made my first out gay friend, Will. Early on, Will told me about *his* unrequited high school love and how he had cried alone in his high school bathroom. I nagged Will to tell me when his heartbreak had occurred. Turns out, it was around the time I found out about my straight best friend's hookup. We had both cried in a school bathroom within a week of each other.

Will and I were not alone; we were just separated.

The truth is that queer people are never alone because we are a part of something greater than ourselves. There were and are queer people all around us at all times. Silenced queers of the present sitting across from us in the classroom. Empathetic and strong queers of the past rooting us on, guiding us. And, most of all, our queer friends of the future, eagerly waiting for us to arrive. This sense of loneliness, of being unique in our closeted misery, is nothing but a strategic lie. We feel this sense of isolation because we live outside of society's norms. There are systems in place to keep us apart. Because a united fleet of queer youth without shame has the potential to *change everything*.

My life would have been different if I had known, in concrete terms, that while growing up, I was not alone. What if the queer community took on the responsibility of assuring its youngest and most vulnerable members that they are seen and valued, that they have a huge, welcoming community waiting to embrace them? We may not be able to change anyone's actual situation—everyone should be able to come out when and if it is safe and makes sense for them. But given our resources and tools of communication, we should be able to band together to create a movement so loud and joyful we'd be impossible to miss. What if taking care of one another and offering solutions to those in need was simply a fundamental part of queer culture?

I was born queer and Jewish. Both of these communities have rich cultures, but I refer to Judaism as my heritage. Heritage most often refers to a person's cultural traditions, histories, and lore passed down from their parents. It can be biological, but it doesn't have to be. In my case, my heritage is Jewish because I was born into a Jewish family. Heritage can also be something you grow into and find on your own. I'd like for you to take a second and identify your heritage. It can be ethnic, religious, geographic, political, or more as long as it makes sense to you.

Being born into my family meant that Jewish culture, knowledge, and ideology were instilled in me by osmosis. Just by being awake, I was taught to be Jewish. My upbringing, while sometimes complicated and often intense, is something I am grateful for. It made me the person I am today.

There is only one problem: I am not only Jewish. I am Jewish and queer. And while my life was overflowing with information about one of my cultures, it was completely devoid of information about the other.

I had never seen a person come out before in real life, on TV, or on the Internet. I had no example to follow and no idea what I was doing. In fact, after my clumsy, and relatively dramatic, exit from the closet, I found myself lonelier than ever. I had no gay friends and no idea where to find them—let alone sex, a relationship, or any feeling of belonging.

In college, my anxiety was through the roof, and I wasn't sleeping well. I'd usually wake up burnt out and hazy. On the days I didn't have class, I'd stay in bed until a friend came to visit or my mother called. On one of those calls, I admitted to her that I really hated being gay. My mom surprised me by saying, "That makes perfect sense, but it is too early to make that decision." She said it was like a Jewish person who had only experienced anti-Semitism deciding they hated being Jewish before eating a matzo ball.

And she was right. Up until this point, I had only experienced the negative parts of queerness. She assured me that once I experienced the positive parts, like joining a community to call my own, finding a partner, and celebrating Pride, I would love being gay. In those early days, I didn't know that being queer meant that I was part of a powerful lineage. At the time, it meant being anxious and bad at sports—and also lots of secret masturbation.

Queers, like the Jews (and many, many others), have a culture with ancient roots. Like all communities, we have ancestors, traditions, and a history of our own. In every single culture throughout history, there is evidence of people experiencing same-sex love, being born intersex, and expressing nonbinary genders and other aspects of queerness. Queerness is a human trait like no other: ever present, inerasable, and entirely invincible. If you wiped out every single queer person, more queer people would just be born tomorrow.

But even though we have always been here, our history can be hard to access. The reason I didn't know anything about my queer history or identity was because nobody taught it to me. Lessons on Jewish history were everywhere. Lessons on queer history were nowhere. Every few months my grandmother would look up from her newspaper and say to us, "Did you know that an astonishing amount of Nobel Prize winners are Jewish? Jewish people have such brilliant minds." When my parents gave me my first cell phone, I wish someone had mentioned the brilliant mind of Sophie Wilson, a trans engineer who designed the Acorn RISC Machine in 1983, one of the most successful IP cores ever, now found in almost every smartphone made in the twenty-first century.

In most cases, history is often passed down from generation to generation. Simply put, we are taught about our heritage from an early age because our ancestors are our biological family. As queer people, a lot of us have complications when it comes to having children biologically. We know for sure that there will always be another generation of queer kids. However, we have no guarantee that queer generations will cross paths, learn from, or even meet one another.

What also factors in to the absence of queer history is queer erasure. This is when mainstream society tries to remove queerness from the record books. Throughout my childhood I was taught endlessly about Sandy Koufax, a professional baseball player who refused to pitch a game of the World Series on the Jewish holiday of Yom Kippur, but was never taught about Alan Turing, the gay mathematician who cracked the Nazi Enigma code, which helped end World War II. It took Queen Elizabeth II sixty-one years to grant Turing a royal pardon for his convictions of "gross indecency," and it took me trolling Wikipedia after eighteen years of education to finally read his name.

The elimination of our culture can be veiled, like a lesson plan that erases queer people from history, but it can also present itself in more sinister, apparent ways. Queer people, like Jewish people, have faced extraordinary violence, oppression, and prejudice. Our history is often erased by the same people who try to physically erase us. The Nazis burned Magnus Hirschfeld's library at the Institute for Sexual Science, and sent queer people to the death camps. Other times, our stories are destroyed by loved ones to preserve the family name, or by ourselves for our own safety. And, in general, history is often written by cisgender men who believe that stories of queer sex and love are inconsequential.

But just because nobody says it out loud doesn't mean it is not true. The history of our people is all around us. You just have to train your eye to see it. Every major museum has works by queer artists. Leonardo da Vinci struggled deeply with the way the church treated him and other homosexuals, but created masterpieces. Every hospital you enter was made possible by the work of queer doctors and nurses. Florence Nightingale revolutionized medicine and challenged society's limitations of what women could do. When you eat peanuts, give a shout-out to George Washington Carver, whose revolutionary farming techniques led to the peanut being commercially available to consumers around the world. Every library contains volumes of work by queer people. Every delegation, grand prize, publication, profession, curriculum, institution, and sport contains a piece of queer history that is yours to be proud of.

Queer people have made important contributions to the world, and being queer means that you are a link in a long chain of people who have accomplished extraordinary things in the face of tremendous peril. You may not be able to feel it yet, but that spirit of queer resilience and survival lives in you.

We are all born into a world that already has a set of rules. Those rules, in the majority of the world, say that boys behave a certain way and girls behave a certain way. As queer people, we are required to break or bend these rules to be our authentic selves. This could be something small, like showing interest in a different game on the playground, or something more significant, like kissing a person of the same sex. Society teaches us that straying from these rules is wrong and has consequences. These consequences range from a disapproving look to social discomfort to missed opportunities, violence, and sometimes death. So, for a time, many of us try to keep our authentic selves a secret.

These secrets birth a powerful weapon called shame. It is heard in our own heads, in our own voices, as we question who we really are. Shame is calculating, manipulative, and violent. Shame often wears a disguise, kindled from the mouths of loved ones who gently push us toward "more traditional choices" in order to "make our lives easier." It comes from places that are meant to be safe, like houses of worship and classrooms. It comes from ourselves.

Society's rules are no secret, and they have been ingrained in us since birth. These rules were not written by queer people and they were not written to help queer people. We already have our own history, culture, accomplishments, and peoplehood. So why are we still abiding by someone else's rules?

Our generation of queers finds themselves in a unique historical position. We have more societal acceptance and legal protections than ever before. We have the ability to communicate with one another in ways that we never have, making us truly a global entity. Yet it is still illegal to be gay in more than seventy countries. Seventy-five countries have laws prohibiting the right to change your gender identity. And amid this progress, queer hate crimes are on the rise in America and all over the world.

It is my dream that the queer community adopts a new set of rules. A set of rules that centers what queer people have in common with one another. A set of rules that positions queer people as players on the same team. A set of rules that uses our hard-won progress as a road map to a brighter, more welcoming world. A world where coming out is less painful and where fewer of us cry in the bathroom alone. A world where governments are met with a colossal and unified global resistance when they try to murder their queer citizens.

I believe that the queer community can foster an environment where it is seen as cool, socially desirable, and even *expected* that we look out for one another. This new culture of united action would be a safety net in times of crisis. And in times of peace it would ensure our community is a place of welcome, warmth, and joy. It will also ensure that we become and remain a safe haven for queer youth and newly out folks. It is my dream that this attitude become a cornerstone of queer life, identity, and culture.

Let us be the standard of generosity and loyalty that all other people aspire to meet. Let us be a nation that shines like the brightest star in a constellation, spreading light to all those around it.

It is my personal belief that this will be possible if we come to this simple understanding:

Queer people anywhere are responsible for queer people everywhere.

In order for our community to adopt this mentality, some major changes must happen. First and foremost:

1.

We approach all queer people with the principles of identification and kindness.

The golden rule—treat others how you want to be treated—is simply not good enough. People who have spent years, possibly their whole lives, being treated as less than or unequal often lack self-worth. I've met a lot of queer people who simply don't know just how special they are and how wonderfully they should be treated.

Allow me to introduce the platinum rule: Treat everyone how you want your best friend to be treated. Go ahead and think of the person you love most in the world. Maybe it is your mom, a partner, a beloved little cousin—someone you are proud of but also worry about. Someone whose future you are actively invested in. I am asking you to approach every queer person you meet the same way you approach them.

I am confident that the way we experience queerness will change if we alter the way we approach one another. When I meet a new queer person, I have a tendency to size them up. I wonder, and proceed to make assumptions, about their relationship status, social media following, confidence in their identity, and personal style. For a long time, and sometimes still today, my gut tells me to treat other queer people with hesitation.

It may take some work, especially for shy folks, but what if our initial reactions upon meeting one another were joy, kindness, and the benefit of the doubt? What if we were just absurdly nice to one another?

When I meet a new queer person, I actively try to remember that we are on the same team. While this person has a different story than mine, it is likely that there is some overlap in our experiences. I tell myself that even if they don't want to be my friend, I should look for ways to be kind or helpful, because I know how tough it is to be queer sometimes.

Our newest members are often in particular need of this type of radical empathy.

2.

Treat newly out people with a particular kindness and understanding.

For the folks that are already out, here's the double diamond platinum rule: Do not take advantage of inexperienced queer people in any capacity! It is natural that newly out folks may lack confidence and self-knowledge. We never use that to our own advantage, and we protect them from anyone trying to do so.

Instead, we do our best to make new members feel comfortable while giving them whatever space they may need. We instill a sense of belonging and self-worth by being patient and endlessly encouraging. We create safe spaces where they can talk to us about the challenges they are facing and how we can identify or help. If they ask, "Why are you being so nice to me?," you can simply respond, "Because I wish someone had been this nice to me." Hopefully one day someone will respond, "Because someone was very nice to me when I first came out, and I hope that one day soon you will pass on the same kindness."

Newly out people are the future of our movement, peoplehood, and culture. What they do, how they feel about being queer, and how involved they are directly impacts the trajectory of our community. Aside from being the right thing to do, it is in our best interest for new members to feel loved, a sense of belonging, and an eagerness to build a bright queer future.

3.

Allow people to come out on their own terms.

We do not expose someone's queerness without their permission. If we see someone who we believe is closeted, it is our obligation to act in a way that would make them feel most comfortable. When a person does come out, we welcome them with open arms. Because the best time to come out is the exact moment you feel most ready.

We do not question other people's sexualities. Instead, we put all that time and effort into creating a community that is so warm and welcoming, folks will be bursting out of the closet to come and join us.

4.

Recognize that the playing field is not equal.

All queer people are created equal, but the world does not treat us that way. Certain identities, queer or not, come with certain privileges. People of color, the trans community, the gender non-conforming community, and disabled people (or any combination of these) face challenges that their white, cisgender, and traditionally abled counterparts do not.

This lesson is often learned the hard way—through personal experience. My first cousin Madison is trans. In addition to sharing a last name and a brilliant grandmother, we have a lot in common. We are both white and Jewish, and grew up in liberal cities. We both came out during our freshman years of college. We share interests, friends, and sometimes clothes. But despite our similarities, our experiences of being queer are very different.

As a transgender woman, Madison faces challenges that I simply do not as a cis gay man. I can shed my queerness and present as straight (as long as I don't talk too much). Madison did not have that privilege early in her transition. Before she "passed" as a cis woman, she was often harassed on the street.

To this day, if Madison and I are attacked for being queer, the chances of Madison's attack ending in murder are much higher. This is only one example. As a cis man, I have easier access to employment, health care, housing, physical safety, sexual partners, and resources than most trans women. This is particularly true for Black trans women, who are significantly more likely to be victims of fatal hate crimes than white trans folk.

The first step is looking inward and recognizing our own privilege. I've found that this is when things start to go awry. Usually, people have two reactions when they realize their own privilege. The first reaction is denial, and the second is guilt, both of which are ultimately a waste of time.

A few weeks after Madison came out, we went to the Audre Lorde Project to get her started on hormones. I was so excited for Madison to take this step, and overjoyed that I got to be a part of her big day. Madison was, understandably, really nervous and not having it with my enthusiasm. Eventually she turned to me and said, "You just don't get it."

My first reaction was denial; how could she say I didn't understand the hardships of being queer? She knew how religious my family was and the challenges I had faced growing up gay. The doctor came into the room and the appointment began. With her typical grace, Madison did her best to navigate through questions that most seventeen-year-olds would be unequipped to answer. The guilt hit me as I realized she was correct: I didn't get it and I never would. My queerness did not call on me to make physical changes to my body without my parents' permission. Being a trans youth was simply an entirely different arena of queerness. While I could empathize, I certainly didn't get it. I stayed silent for the rest of the appointment.

On our walk back to the subway, I turned to Madison and apologized. I told her, "You are right, I don't get it. I am sorry for acting inappropriately. How can I best be of service? I am here for you."

5.

The more privileged members of our society must rally behind the less privileged.

Once we recognize our privilege, the next question must be: How do we leverage our privilege and our resources for the benefit of all members of our community—specifically, the most vulnerable? How do we break down the systems that granted us these unearned privileges to begin with?

Historically, the opposite has happened—marginalized groups have tended to rally behind the more privileged. Stonewall, the event which many say launched the gay liberation movement, was started and primarily fought by queer people of color, street-hustling effeminate gay youth, trans women, butch lesbians, and gender non-conforming folks. However, once the fires of the riot had gone out, it was gay men, benefiting from male privilege, who took control of the movement throughout the 1970s.

By the mid-'80s, the gay male community was immobilized by the AIDS crisis. But huge numbers of women showed up to help. Women, queer and not, played a key role in the success of ACT UP (AIDS Coalition to Unleash Power)—the activist group that emerged in 1987 to fight the AIDS crisis.

At the height of the crisis, HIV positive gay men were in desperate need of blood transfusions, but all gay men were barred from donating. So a group of lesbians in San Diego banded together and created a group called the Blood Sisters. Starting in 1983, they organized regular blood drives and set up systems so folks could apply for the type of blood they needed.

Our community's circumstance may have changed, but the urgency for direct action remains the same.

It is imperative that we pool our resources and strength behind queer groups that are most vulnerable today. This includes but is not limited to trans folks, people of color, American Indians, refugees, immigrants, asylum seekers, youth, elderly folks, intersex children, and gender non-conforming people. Those who exist at the intersection of these identities, like a trans person of color or an intersex asylum seeker, face even greater danger. For many, leaving the house is a life-and-death decision.

A fundamental principle of Jewish law and culture is "pikuach nefesh," or "to save a life." The concept is simple: Saving a life takes priority over all other considerations. When a human life is in jeopardy, almost every other law and religious practice goes out the window.

This same concept can be applied to strengthen the queer community. We must prioritize and protect our most marginalized members, those whose lives are at the greatest risk. The freer we are, the more responsibility we have.

6.

Ask "What can I do to help?"
and listen to the answer.

Showing up for a marginalized group that you don't exactly identify with can be daunting. The key to success is listening and learning. I have found that the best course of action is to read and learn as much as possible about the group you'd like to support and the issues they face. Then, when you show up, kindly introduce yourself and volunteer to be of service when the opportunity arises. Deciding to help a group of people without their input can be dangerous. We already have enough misinformation and misrepresentation to fight.

Every queer person has their own story with their own unique blend of challenges. That means everyone can only truly understand, speak to, and represent their own experience. You can offer advice and resources, but ultimately, only someone who has directly experienced an issue can be in the best position to provide a solution.

That means we have no opinions on other people's queerness. Let's repeat that, for folks in the back: We do not qualify, deny, or question a person's belonging to the queer community. No one queer experience is more valid than another.

It can be difficult to feel a sense of unity if your stories are not the same. This is not exclusive to just queer folks. No culture or group of people share a single lived experience.

Which brings me to my next point:

7.

LGBTQIAA+ people should work in solidarity with all oppressed people.

Progress is made when we band together. On August 12, 2017, Heather Heyer was murdered in Charlottesville, Virginia, during a riot that was born out of a white supremacist rally. That evening, we took to the streets in New York. Showing solidarity was easy and obvious: White supremacists hate people who are Black, Muslim, Asian, queer, immigrants, and more. Their gathering was a direct threat against all of us. While sometimes less obvious, our intersecting interests are always there when a marginalized group is attacked.

For example, on January 27, 2017, President Donald Trump enacted Executive Order 13769, otherwise known as the "Muslim Ban." This effectively closed America's doors to refugees, asylum seekers, and visitors from seven majority-Muslim countries. By midday, thousands of protesters had descended on airports and courthouses around the country. I joined the protests without thinking twice about it. My great-grandparents sought asylum in America because of anti-Semitic violence they experienced in Russia. The majority of the Jewish people I know are only around today because their ancestors escaped the Nazis by restarting in America.

Throughout my Jewish education, I was taught the phrase "Never Again" in regard to the Holocaust. It felt like an alarm went off in my head as I watched our government attack an already vulnerable religious minority group by removing this lifesaving mechanism. This felt like the moment we had trained for in Hebrew school: Never again was now. I grabbed my kippah and took to the streets.

At the time, I didn't understand that we were showing up not just for the Muslim community, but for the queer community, too. Each of the banned countries had outlawed homosexuality and made it incredibly dangerous to live as an out and proud citizen. Punishment for homosexuality ranges from one year in prison to the death penalty. In three of the seven countries, it is illegal to change one's gender identity. There are queer refugees and asylum seekers in those countries looking for a way out, and we march for them, too.

Showing up for other marginalized groups by

going to protests, donating money, and sharing resources is not a selfless act or charity. It is the key to our continued survival. A world that is less racist, less Islamophobic, and less ableist will be less queerphobic and vice versa. Hatred and intolerance are nothing but the fear of people who are different from you. By combating one type of hatred, you combat all types of hatred.

I understand that this sounds like a big ask and a lot of responsibility. It is! But a cultural shift is just a fancy term for a group of people committing to tiny changes over the course of time.

8.

**We have limited time and resources—
let's use them to lift each other up.**

It is important to note that a key tool of oppression is turning marginalized groups against one another or against themselves. It is easier to encourage people to tear themselves apart than to tear them apart yourself.

For example, in the death camps, the Nazis recruited prisoners who were called *kapos*. In exchange for better living conditions and food—essentially a better chance of survival—the kapos brutally enforced the Nazis' rules. The kapos were often just as violent as the SS guards, as their positions were tenuous, and relied on the SS guards' satisfaction with their work. The usage of kapos allowed the camps to run with fewer paid guards and created irrevocable damage to both the prisoners and the kapos themselves. When a fellow Jew could turn on you at any time, nobody (and nowhere) was safe.

Even in less extreme times, every culture and peoplehood experience a degree of infighting. Creating a movement within any given community is inherently chaotic. There will always be a wide array of conflicting opinions. And we should absolutely create space for debate and conversation, to consistently look inward at the divisions and problems within our own community. *But* it is equally important to find what unites us, and to remember that at the end of the day, we have the same goals in mind. As a founder and card-carrying member of Gays Against Guns, I was initially disturbed when I heard about the Pink Pistols—a gay gun rights group whose slogan reads: "Armed Gays Don't Get Bashed."

I very quickly learned that they were trying to do the same exact thing we were—make the world a safer place for queer people. We just had really (*really*) different ways of getting there. I'll never agree with their policies or partner with their group. I also won't spend too much time attacking or trying to discredit them. That only takes away time and resources that could be used fighting for reasonable gun control. Activist group Queer Nation says in its manifesto: "Let yourself be angry." Let's make sure to use that weapon, that anger, and that power on our oppressors, not one another.

9.

Support queer people whenever possible, wherever possible.

Growing up, I watched my family make decisions every day that were informed by our community. I remember when a kosher restaurant opened down the street and we went twice in a week, even though the food wasn't great. My mom explained that we "do our best to support Jewish businesses."

When possible, and within reason, I'd recommend that queer people do the same thing. Let's do our best to support queer-owned businesses and initiatives. If we are donating money in light of a natural disaster, find an organization that is queer-friendly. If you are donating clothing, consider the local LGBTQIAA+ youth center.

Showing up, applauding, and supporting queer people is a radical and vital act of self-love in a world that constantly tells us we are not enough.

10.

You can be closeted and still do this work.
You can be straight and do this work.

Despite my exuberant femininity, I was never really bullied. My interpersonal skills combined with my crew of macho and popular brothers gave me enough social capital to get by relatively unscathed. I know that not everyone is so lucky. One year at sleepaway camp, there was another queer boy who got his fair share of teasing, and to my regret, I went along with the group.

It is not fair to ask a closeted, but slightly more popular boy to stand in front of his whole bunk and demand that they not call someone gay. That is not entirely realistic, and also maybe not the world's best idea. But I certainly didn't have to join in on the teasing. In the many moments that summer when he wasn't being teased, I absolutely had the time to show him some extra kindness. Looking back, there are about a million things that I could have done to help him have a better summer without putting myself in a dangerous or even uncomfortable situation.

You don't need to be out or queer to purchase queer books, read them, and donate them to your local library or LGBTQIAA+ center. You don't need to be out or queer to lend a kind ear to a suffering queer person at school. You don't need to be out or queer to tell someone you really like their Trans Pride shirt. You don't have to be out or queer to vote for a politician with inclusive policies. You certainly don't have to be out or queer to show a little extra love for a marginalized group.

I wish our ancestors could see us now. I know they would be shocked at what we have been able to accomplish in the last fifty or so years.

Unfortunately, progress is not a promise and liberation is not linear. Freedoms are often taken quicker than they are given. Supreme Court Justice Ruth Bader Ginsburg said, "My dear spouse used to say the true symbol of the US is not a bald eagle. It is the pendulum. And when it goes very far in one direction you can count on it coming back."

On June 12, 2016, forty-nine people were murdered at Pulse, a queer nightclub in Orlando, Florida. In America, and in so many parts of the world, the pendulum is swinging backward.

The queer movement is only one of many causes

subject to the tides of history. We cannot always control how and when the pendulum will swing. We can only control how we react.

We, as a community, have been born into a world that has not been designed for us. We know that hate does not discriminate. It has shockingly low standards for its choice of subject. Hatred is a disease, and if untreated, it becomes contagious. Those who hate one queer hate them all. Those who stand up for one queer must stand up for us all.

The queer people, like the Jewish people, are a diaspora—scattered in every corner of the Earth.

Today, we have members of the queer family living in every single corner, community, and country in the world, all fighting for the same cause. Only now we have the means to communicate with one another, and members with actual privilege and leverage to lift us. Our generation has the liberties and tools no generation of queers has ever had before. We have the opportunity to unite and create a New Queer Conscience.

Queer people anywhere are responsible for queer

people everywhere. Queer people anywhere must fight for queer people everywhere. After all, wouldn't you want someone to fight for you?

RESOURCES

Organizations to Join and Support

ACT UP: A diverse, nonpartisan group of individuals united in anger and committed to direct action to end the AIDS crisis. www.actupny.org

The Anti-Violence Project: This organization empowers lesbian, gay, bisexual, transgender, queer, and HIV-affected communities and allies to end all forms of violence through organizing and education, and supports survivors through counseling and advocacy. www.avp.org

#BreakThePatent: An activist group that aims to break the pharmaceutical company Gilead Science's patent on the lifesaving HIV drug Truvada to make it available for everyone. www.breakthepatent.org

The Dru Project: A nonprofit organization created to honor Christopher Andrew Leinonen and his partner, Juan Ramon Guerrero, whose lives were taken at Pulse nightclub in Orlando, Florida. The Dru Project provides scholarships and created the country's most comprehensive gay-straight alliance guidebook. www.thedruproject.org

Gays Against Guns: An inclusive direct action group of LGBTQ people and their allies committed to nonviolently breaking the gun industry's chain of death—investors, manufacturers, the NRA, and politicians who block safer gun laws. www.gaysagainstguns.net

interACT: An organization that uses innovative legal strategies to advocate for the human rights of children born with intersex traits. www.interactadvocates.org

Intersex Justice Project (IJP): A group that seeks the end of medically invasive and unnecessary surgeries in the United States that target intersex children and adolescents by empowering intersex people of color to advance that change. www.intersexjusticeproject.org

Immigration Equality: A leading national LGBTQ immigrant rights organization. www.immigrationequality.org

RUSA LGBT: A network for Russian-speaking LGBTQ individuals, their friends, supporters, and loved ones. www.rusalgbt.com

SAGE: The country's largest and oldest organization dedicated to improving the lives of older LGBT people people. www.sageusa.org

The Stonewall Foundation: A community foundation for lesbian, gay, bisexual, transgender, queer, and ally donors, volunteers, and grant- and scholarship-seekers. www.stonewallfoundation.org

Voices 4: Nonviolent direct action activist group with chapters in Berlin, London, and New York. The group's motto is: "When you mess with one queer, you mess with us all." @voices4_

ABOUT US

Pocket Change Collective was born out of a need for space. Space to think. Space to connect. Space to be yourself. And this is your invitation to join us.

These books are small, but they are mighty. They ask big questions and propose even bigger solutions. They show us that no matter where we come from or where we're going, we can all take part in changing the communities around us. Because the possibilities of how we can use our space for good are endless.

So thank you. Thank you for picking this book up. Thank you for reading. Thank you for being a part of the Pocket Change Collective.